Feng Shui in a Day

**just
try
this**

Feng Shui in a Day

Barb Rogers

Red Wheel
Boston, MA / York Beach, ME

First published in 2005 by
Red Wheel/Weiser, LLC
York Beach, ME
With offices at:
368 Congress Street
Boston, MA 02210
www.redwheelweiser.com

LIBRARY OF CONGRESS CATALOGING-IN-PUBLICATION DATA
Rogers, Barb,
  Feng shui in a day / Barb Rogers.
    p. cm.
  ISBN 1-59003-073-7
  1. Feng shui. I. Title.
  BF1779.F4R64 2005
  133.3'337—dc22

                          2004014130

Typeset in Mrs. Eaves and Dalliance by Kathleen Wilson Fivel
Printed in Canada
TCP

12 11 10 09 08 07 06 05
  8 7 6 5 4 3 2 1

To my husband and best friend, Tom Rogers Jr.,
without whose support and love none of this would be
possible. Thank you for your patience as I rearranged
everything in the house and hung crystals and bamboo
flutes over your head. I know you were afraid that if you
stood still long enough, I'd hang a crystal around your neck.
All my love, all my thanks.

Contents

just
try
this

Introduction

*J*ust as a mixture of blood and oxygen flows through our bodies to keep us healthy and vital, an energy called "chi" flows through and rejuvenates our living space. When our balance is off, we become sick, unable to thrive. The same thing can happen to our apartment, cottage, or twenty-five-room mansion when the flow of chi is unbalanced or blocked. Healthier living through doctor visits, proper diet, exercise, and medication can fix the body, and spirituality can heal the soul. So what can we do for our homes?

Feng Shui (pronounced *fung shway*) is the ancient Chinese art of placement. It uses colors, numbers, and directions to determine a position for each item in our environment that will best activate universal energy, or chi, and optimize the results of our life goals. The better the flow of chi in your surroundings, the more balance, peace, good health, and prosperity you will have in your life. In Feng Shui, the desired effect is to have chi move gently through each room of your living space, around your furniture, and back out. You don't want it moving too fast or too slow. If it moves too quickly, you will not get the benefits, and if it moves too slowly, it becomes stale and settled, inhibiting opportunities in your life.

The earliest recorded reference to Feng Shui goes back to the Han Dynasty in 202 BC. The theory was used as protection against the elements and unwanted visitors. Feng Shui actually means "wind and water," which probably referred to where to build a home with protection from the wind and a decent water supply nearby. Those things were as important to them as our plumbing and electricity are to us today.

Needless to say, things have changed a bit since then. So unless you are buying land or building the house you'll live in, there is no need to go into the earliest forms of Feng Shui. Most of us already have our living space and just need some practical advice on the basic concepts of Feng Shui that are fast, cheap, and easy to apply. It doesn't cost much to move a bed, and if it could actually make a difference, wouldn't it be worth the effort? Feng Shui is a lot like spirituality. We don't have to understand how it works; we simply open our mind, try it, and see what happens.

Before You Begin

Before you start with Feng Shui, the first thing you need to consider is your environment's "cholesterol." In your living space, cholesterol is dirt, dust, and clutter. You can't achieve Feng Shui in a day if your place is dirty and filled with items that slow the chi down. Clean it up, or the only thing you'll have is *sha*—stale or bad energy lying around, stuck in the muck. If your life is in the same condition, your home's cholesterol level may have something to do with it.

Got your place tidy? Then the next thing to consider is what you wish to achieve through Feng Shui. Do you have health issues, relationship problems, or financial concerns? Are you having trouble conceiving a child or dealing with your neighbors? Or are you simply seeking a balance in your life, which will ultimately affect all other situations?

You won't need many supplies. What you'll be doing most is moving around what you already have—furniture, pictures, figurines, mirrors, and plants. If you find you can't move something, there are easy fixes. The only things you'll need are a few crystals, which can be found at garage sales, junk stores, and the like; bamboo flutes, which can be found on cheap bamboo chimes; some candles; and inexpensive chimes.

Chimes can be made of many different materials, including wood, metal, ceramic, baked clay, and glass. It's important to be aware of what the chime is made of so that you can place it in the right location according to the Creative Cycle of Elements. You don't want to hang white metal chimes in the south area of a room because rather than helping the chi to flow, they will repel it or bring in sha.

I brought my chimes in, cleaned them and hung them in the appropriate areas, removed crystals from an old lamp, and already had candles for emergencies. All I had to purchase were two red candles.

Items from rummage sales and junk stores are in a special category. I've read you should lay your hand on the item and feel its vibrations. I'm not sure I'm that sensitive to vibrations, but it might work for you. I purchase things that are visually appealing and would suit my house. Once home, I leave my treasures outside and burn sage around them. If there is any "evil" in them, the smell of sage will choke it right out. Then I keep them outside overnight.

Once you have figured out what you want to accomplish and have your supplies in hand, you are ready to identify the eight directions in your home.

The Eight Directions

Directions have always been difficult for me. To orient myself, I began by purchasing a small, inexpensive compass. I also did some association. Where does the sun rise? In the east. Which walls in my home are in the east? I did the same associations with the sunset. Finally, since I live in a small mountain community in Arizona, I associated north with Prescott and south with Phoenix. If I know the four major directions, the others aren't hard to figure out.

Once you've figured out where you are in relation to the sun, other towns, or whatever landmarks or elements you've chosen, take a walk through your living space. It doesn't matter if it's an efficiency apartment or a ten-room house; each room is a world of its own, and the door to the room is the entrance to that world. If you want to focus on one specific problem, you may only need to work on one room or area. I promise you, though: once you begin to practice Feng Shui, it's hard to stop.

As you walk through your space, pay attention to the Eight Directions Chart (see page 15) and the two Cycle of Elements charts (see pages 16–17). The Eight Directions Chart tells you which colors, numbers, elements, and issues are associated with each direction, which will guide you in moving furniture and other personal items into a creative cycle.

In the center of the Eight Directions Chart is the symbol for Yin and Yang. Yin is black and depicts negative influences. Yang is white and represents positive influences. It is necessary to have a balance of both in our lives to find harmony. For instance, pain seems like a negative. However, if we didn't feel pain, we would be unaware that something was wrong with our bodies. This same idea translates to our living environment. Imagine you're driving home. Do you feel like you are going to a comforting haven or would you rather just keep driving past it? If it's the latter, you're getting the same message that a severe pain gives you when something isn't right in your body—something isn't right in your living space. With some very simple changes using Feng Shui principles, you could create a place of balance and harmony—a true sanctuary.

When you stand in the entrance to any room, hold the Eight Directions Chart flat, with the direction of the doorway toward your body. Once you know what direction you're standing in, the chart will tell you where all your other directions are. Compare your room and your objectives with the colors, numbers, and goals listed on the chart.

For instance, look to the south. Is there anything associated with water on, or near, your south wall? South is fire, and water puts out fire. That picture of the ocean may be inhibiting you from reaching your goal of fame or fortune. To ignite the fire, remove the picture and perhaps replace it with sconces holding red candles, or another picture of a landscape with just a splash of red in it . . . a barn or a bush. Red, in the south, especially if it's combined with the number nine, can bring great luck and acknowledgment. If you don't want nine statues, candles, or pictures, try stringing nine red beads onto a wire or thread and hanging them on the wall. You don't have to use large, obvious objects; you simply need to apply the right numbers and colors in the right areas.

If you are more interested in attaining, or reviving, a relationship than achieving fame or fortune, focus on the southwest area. If you want to be two instead of one, put it out there.

If you want to bring a family together and improve health, move three green plants to the east. If you want to bring in more wealth, invoke the southeast dynamics by combining four purple items—say, a statue or vase with a purple feather, plus three purple stones.

The Cycle charts will aid you in the process of attaining your goals. From the Eight Directions Chart, determine the element that corresponds to the direction you're working. Then refer to the Creative Cycle of Elements chart to see what other element strengthens the effect of your direction element. For example, the element for the southwest is earth. According to the Creative Cycle of Elements chart, fire makes earth. So when you choose the container for your two roses, think baked clay. The clay comes from the earth and it has been baked or "fired" to create the pot.

The Destructive Cycle of Elements chart tells you what not to put next to your direction element. For instance, if you're going place a fountain in the north corner of a room to symbolize the water element, don't place a potted plant next to it. Earth (dirt) muddies the water.

Remember, don't complicate it. For instance, if you see a need for purple in the southeast area of a room, that doesn't mean you have to paint your wall purple, hang purple drapes, or add a garish purple chair. It's enough to add a purple figurine, a purple stone, or a piece of art with purple hues in it. Many of us have everything we need but in the wrong places. Look around this room, other rooms, even closets, and pull out the item that will complete your creative cycle.

If you are confused about the water element, as I was, know that you don't have to put fountains in every room. A picture with water in it, or anything associated with water, such as a watering can or seashells, will suffice. I put sea salt in a small black container in the north, but placing a seashell and black stone together can accomplish the same thing.

It's time to begin. You are about to embark on some simple changes that can bring great results in your life. I hope you're as excited as I am. Some say you should watch for subtle changes, be aware of little things. Not so for me. I made drastic Feng Shui changes to my whole house and expected dramatic results—and I got them. If you expect little, that's what you'll get. Set your sights on the stars.

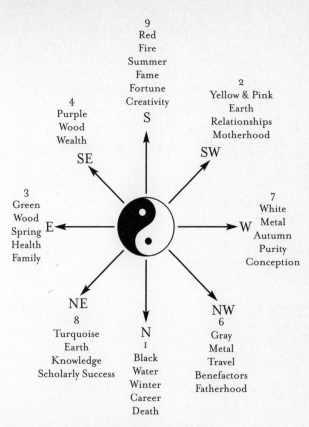

9
Red
Fire
Summer
Fame
Fortune
Creativity
S

2
Yellow & Pink
Earth
Relationships
Motherhood
SW

4
Purple
Wood
Wealth
SE

3
Green
Wood
Spring
Health
Family
E

7
White
Metal
Autumn
Purity
Conception
W

8
Turquoise
Earth
Knowledge
Scholarly Success
NE

1
Black
Water
Winter
Career
Death
N

6
Gray
Metal
Travel
Benefactors
Fatherhood
NW

EIGHT DIRECTIONS CHART

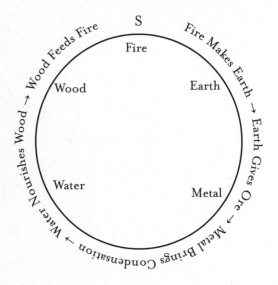

S

Fire

Wood

Earth

Water

Metal

Wood Feeds Fire

Fire Makes Earth → Earth Gives Ore

Water Nourishes Wood →

Metal Brings Condensation ←

CREATIVE CYCLE OF ELEMENTS CHART

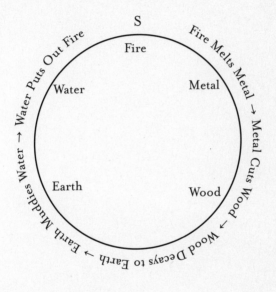

DESTRUCTIVE CYCLE OF ELEMENTS CHART

The Main Entrance

*R*emember the last time you had a head cold? Remember that terrible feeling of not being able to breathe well? When you can't breathe well, it drains your energy, makes you lethargic and miserable. Imagine your main entrance as the nose to your house. The lack of good, flowing chi could affect your house the way the lack of oxygen affects your body.

Anything that blocks the main entrance or causes confusion there will stifle the flow of energy into your house or apartment. The address or apartment number should be clearly marked; if you have more than one door, the main entrance should be set apart so there is no question about which door is which. You don't want opportunity knocking on someone else's door when it is clearly meant for you.

If you happen to live in an apartment or a house with an attached garage, and you use a connecting inside door for convenience and safety, do not consider that to be your main entrance. Focus on your front door, and open it at least once a day. There may be some really good chi swirling around it with no other way to get in.

A south-facing front door is best and can bring great blessings to you. If you can, paint it red. If you can't, hang something on it that has a splash of red in it such as a wreath with red berries or your name or house number painted red.

No matter which direction your front door faces, keep it in good repair and the area around it clean and tidy. A round or oval doormat is more inviting to guests, but no matter the shape, keep it swept, and shake it once in a while.

Stairs leading up to your main entrance can make it more difficult for the flow of chi to enter, and it may exit much more quickly. Place a potted plant at the foot of the stairs and a crystal about halfway between the door and bottom of the staircase. If you have a light fixture, keep it in good repair, with the bulb working, and perhaps hang your crystal from it.

A basement apartment, where you must go down some steps to enter, could trap chi until it gets old and stale. To keep the chi moving, try using a wind chime halfway down the stairs or near the door. Be sure to keep the stairway well lit. Whether you are forced to go up or down a staircase to reach your main entrance, a mirror placed at the landing can draw good chi to it.

If your front door opens inward, you might try hanging a small set of chimes or bells above it that tinkles when the top of the door swings open. When shop owners did this in the days before electronic buzzers, the sound not only alerted them to an arriving customer, it brought opportunity to them by moving the chi through the door more quickly. You can do the same in your own home.

Once you've cleared the path for entry into your home, you'll be ready to move to the living room.

Main Entrance
Colors, Numbers, and Elements

The main entrance is not only where chi enters your living space but also where others get their first impression of you. In addition, it affects how you feel about yourself. A door in disrepair, with peeling paint, a loose doorknob, locks that don't work, or just poor lighting can attract bad energy, put opportunity off, stifle creativity, and leave you with negative feelings about your-self. It won't inspire anticipation of a good experience inside either.

Most times we don't have a choice about our house numbers. However, there are some tricks I've learned to change the energy of "negative" numbers. Imagine you are stuck with a number like 666. Some consider this a very evil number. Separating the sixes by placing something in between them can counteract the negative effect. You might have your numbers done on tiles and place two angel tiles in between them. If you have a house number you particularly want to emphasize, paint it a different color.

Consult the Eight Directions Chart and the Cycle of Elements charts to determine what types of pots, mailbox, and even chairs to have near your main entrance.

Quick Tips for the Main Entrance

- If your back door or yard is visible when you open your front door, place a folding screen, beaded curtains, or potted plants in your path to break the line of vision. If that's not possible, hang a crystal inside the front door.
- Avoid clutter around the entrance. Place a container outside for shoes not to be worn in the house.
- If there is a wall directly in front of you as you enter, hang a large mirror so chi isn't trapped.
- If your front door bumps into another door, hang something red—even a piece of string—on each doorknob.
- The entryway should be well lit but with soft lighting.

2

The Living Room

*H*ave you ever wandered into a coffee house, a restaurant, a pub, or a lounge, sat in a comfortable chair, and said to your friends, "I love this place"? Does the conversation flow, the time passing so quickly that you want to return again and again? Now, imagine your living room as a public room. How would it feel if you walked in for the first time?

The living room is the social part of your house. It's where visitors, friends, and family interact. It is your public room. With very little effort, and the help of Feng Shui concepts, you can create that cozy atmosphere that will draw a wealth of friends, encourage family discussions, and bring people together in a convivial setting.

If your living room is rarely used, if visitors dart in and out, if children avoid the public room, you need to look at that area of your home with a Feng Shui eye. What is it about the room that puts people off?

Feng Shui is not about how beautiful or expensive your furnishings are. I've been in some fabulous-looking living rooms and found myself sitting on the edge of a Queen Anne chair ready to bolt at the first opportunity. I've also been in modest dwellings with well-used furniture and happily sipped coffee for hours.

Your living room tells people not only about your financial status but also about your personality and what is important to you. The quality of your furniture doesn't matter as much as its placement, the color in the room, what artwork you display. I always have problems in stark-white living rooms or rooms with harsh lighting. Unlike

Westerners, the Chinese see white as a color of mourning. If your living-room walls are white, you can offset the cold, sterile feeling by accenting with color in paintings, wall hangings, plants, furniture, curtains, or drapes. Think again: what was it you liked about that public place?

The ideal living room is rectangular-shaped, located in the front of the house, and facing south or east. However, we work with what we have. No matter what the location of your living area, even if it is just part of a larger room, there are some simple things you can change to bring that flow of chi into your life (see diagram on page 38). And if it opens you to many good things, isn't it worth a try?

The southeast area of every room is important because it is associated with good fortune, but the southeast section of the living room is your most powerful wealth area. Wealth can mean many things. It can be a wealth of friends, family, or knowledge, or success in business and career, and it can affect the flow of money into your home. You must decide what your goal is and, using the Eight Directions Chart (see page 15), apply numbers, colors, and directions to your southeast corner. The wealth corner normally contains four purple items. Imagine you wish to incorporate correspondences from the north because you have recently begun a new career. Place the four purple items on a piece of black fabric and add a sea shell. If you are concerned with bringing family together, place a green, woody plant and two pictures of family members grouped together at a happy function with your four purple items.

Whatever you've decided to do in the living room with your wealth corner, pay attention to the Cycle of Elements charts (see pages 16–17). If you've placed a family picture near a woody plant, make sure the picture frame is not metal.

As the Destructive Cycle of Elements chart shows, metal cuts wood and will cancel out all you hoped to achieve. You can correct the cycle by placing a water element between them. Metal makes condensation and water feeds the wood.

Living Room
Colors, Numbers, and Elements

Your living room is like your body. You dress for success, you dress for approachability, you dress to give a certain impression when going out in public. So how will you dress your living room? How will you accessorize your room? What impression do you want to give?

Look at the Directions and Cycles charts to determine what your options are. Move that painting with red in it to the south wall; place your purple African violet in the southeast corner; put that green, leafy plant in the east.

Make sure you arrange elements in the right order to avoid a destructive cycle.

A dark living room can bring feelings of isolation and depression. On the other hand, white and other stark colors such as cool blues and grays can give the room a cold, uninviting feeling. You can fix the darkness with better lighting, of course, and you can fix a stark room by adding warmth through splashes of color in throw pillows, plants, artwork, afghans, and rugs.

If your apartment is a combined living space, try to separate the areas as best you can. If you must sleep in your living room on a pull-out bed, for example, always make it up in the morning. Read the section on bedrooms and combine that advice with advice for the living room. If your living room and dining area occupy the same open space, find a way to separate the two, whether with a folding screen, plants, a beaded curtain, or a fabric swag (see page 39). Every functional area in your home should have its own distinct space.

The most important thing is to know what you want from the room—whether you want to hole up on the couch in a dark room filled with depression, or you desire company, relaxation, wonderful conversation, and a family pulled together because they want to be in that space. It is simply a matter of choice and a bit of effort.

Quick Tips for the Living Room

- Furniture
  - Place tables between guest chairs and the coffee table between the couch and the chairs.
  - The host's back should face the wall, not the door or the window.
  - Don't block the doorway with furniture.
  - Arrange furniture in an octagon or a circle if possible. When all chairs are occupied,

each person should be able to see all of the
others without turning around.
- If furniture has sharp corners and the
corners point to seated guests, either
rearrange the piece or place a cover over it.
- If the couch or easy chairs are sagging,
place a piece of wood under the cushion.
- Make sure wooden chairs are in good
repair.
· Ceilings
- Chi flows down a slanted ceiling, putting
pressure on its lowest point. If you can't
keep from placing furniture under the
low area, place a floor lamp or hang
three crystals.
- To cancel the effect of a beamed ceiling—
beams inhibit the healthy flow of chi—
hang from the beams two hollow bamboo
flutes, chimes, or crystals.

- Fireplace
  - Chi can get lost up the chimney. Place a mirror above the fireplace.
  - Add leafy green plants to both sides, but not woody plants.
- Odd-shaped rooms
  - Raise the chi in a sunken living room by adding floor lamps.
  - Divide an L-shaped living room using a folding screen, plants, a beaded curtain, or a piece of furniture.
- Lighting
  - Avoid harsh lighting or a dark room.
  - Strive for good light, but keep a relaxed atmosphere by using table and floor lamps.
  - Utilize natural light whenever possible.
- Artwork
  - Use vivid or bold artwork.
  - Be conscious of the materials in statues,

frames, and pots for plants so you don't
end up with a destructive element cycle.

- Art in the living room should evoke
  feelings of happiness, growth, and
  vibrant living.
- Never put even a picture of water on a
  south wall.

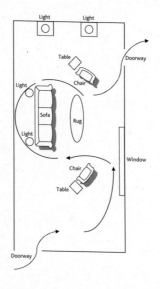

EASY FLOW OF CHI FOR LIVING ROOM

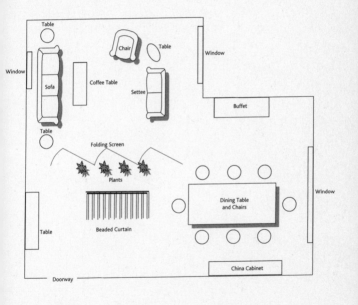

Table

Chair

Table

Window

Window

Sofa

Coffee Table

Settee

Buffet

Table

Folding Screen

Plants

Window

Table

Dining Table
and Chairs

Beaded Curtain

China Cabinet

Doorway

Quick Fix for Living–Dining Room

3 *The Dining Room*

he ideal dining room is located east of the kitchen, is a separate room, has two doors, and is not too close to the front entrance of the house. The east promotes health and growth, which is what nourishing food should give us. A room or space set aside for eating will lend itself to a pleasant dining experience and good conversation with no distractions. Two doors will allow the chi to flow in and out more easily. If the dining room is too close to the front entrance, guests will not linger after a meal, and family members will think of food as soon as they walk through the door.

What if you don't have a separate dining room and instead eat in the kitchen, in the same room as your living room, or in a corner of your small apartment? The same Feng Shui concepts can apply to any eating area. The point is to have an area specified for eating, a space that's inviting and that will encourage family members and guests to linger for conversation afterwards.

Dining Room Elements, Colors, and Numbers

What you wish to achieve through family communications in the dining room will tell you what colors to use and what additions to make. If you have a family member with health problems, place green objects in sets of three to the east. You can use pictures, candles, plants, stones, or a combination as long as you don't break the creative cycle. Placing turquoise and the number eight in the northeast will encourage a student of any age to openly discuss strengths and weaknesses in his or her chosen field.

If your dining area is part of another room, try to separate the two spaces by function. I recently did Feng Shui on a house whose living room and dining room were one long area, with the front door looking straight through to the back door. The first thing we did was paint the outside wall two different colors. The area designated for dining was painted a pale mauve to encourage the owner's relationships and more intimate conversation.

The living room was painted a darker, dusky rose and softened with white lace curtains. At the point the colors met, we painted a dark green stripe. By using two area rugs—one under the small, oval dining table and one in the center of the living area—we gave each part of the room a different look.

From the opposite wall we brought a bamboo folding screen out about a third of the way across the room and placed a large, earthen potted plant in front of it. Suddenly, the stark white, straight-through room felt different. It invited the residents to sit longer, enjoy talking and sipping coffee, and open up to each other in a better way. It has become two rooms, each with a reason for being.

It's important to understand what each room is for and then to utilize it to its best advantage. Cluttering our eating area with bills, unanswered letters, or any other unfinished business can affect our digestion and our ability to nourish our mind and soul as well as our body. Remember, it's all about balance.

Quick Tips for the Dining Room

- Dining area
  - Don't crowd furniture or allow clutter.
  - The table size should not cramp the space.
  - Don't block the door.
  - If the dining area is combined with other spaces, separate, if possible, with plants, a folding screen, a swag of fabric, a beaded curtain, or a piece of furniture.
- Table
  - Octangle, round, or oval shapes are best.
  - If the table is square or rectangular, do not seat anyone at the corners.
- Chairs
  - Make sure chairs are sturdy, well maintained, and comfortable.
  - Use an even number of chairs.
  - Keep the backs of chairs to the walls.

- Artwork
  - Include nothing garish or distracting.
  - Scenic paintings or a mirror that reflects the table are best.

4

The Kitchen

I've read that the living room is the heart of a house, but for me the heart is the kitchen. The quantity and quality of what we eat can affect us physically, emotionally, and spiritually. The foods prepared in our kitchen carry us through the day, make us weak or strong, help us accomplish our tasks, can determine our state of health, and influence the way we look and feel. Food is a powerful source of energy, so careful attention to where it originates and how it's prepared can give us an edge in life. What we choose to put in our body will affect every other room in our house and our lives out into the world.

The kitchen contains two strong elements:

fire (stove) and water (sink). In today's world there are also the microwave (fire) and dishwasher (water) to contend with. If your water elements are too close to the fire elements, you can cause a destructive cycle in the kitchen. There is a simple fix, though. Place something made of wood between the two. A woody plant works better than a cutting board or a picture frame because it is alive. Something metal will work too, but I think wood is best.

If your dining table is in the kitchen, or if you eat at a breakfast bar or table, try placing a living plant in the center of the table or counter to break up the fire/water elements. Pay attention to the dining room chapter for tips about your eating area.

The placement and condition of the fire elements—the stove and microwave—can affect wealth and nourishment. The location and maintenance of the water elements—the sink and dishwasher—can affect the flow of money in and out of your life.

White is the color of purity and mixes well with metal, which is prevalent in the kitchen. If you want a room painted white, this is the one to pick. It doesn't really matter what color your walls are, as long as the kitchen is airy and light. It's where your nourishment for the day begins. If the kitchen is dirty and depressing, it could have implications on the rest of your day.

Kitchen
Colors, Numbers, and Elements

If you're concerned about bringing the family together or the health of family members, the color green, especially in the east, is best. Live plants in the kitchen bring growth and nourishment and break up the fire/water elements. They bring the feeling of spring, a sense of hope, energy, and renewal that can follow you into your workday and put that spring back in your step.

As you look at the Eight Directions Chart (see page 15), you'll see the number three as well as the color green are relevant in the east. Try hanging three pictures of plants, flowers, or trees. You might enhance an east windowsill with three green candles, three live plants, or three green stones. Whatever you decide, remember that the kitchen is where you start out each morning and your experiences there can affect the rest of your day.

Quick Tips for the Kitchen

- Stove
  - Your back should not be to the door while cooking. If so, hang a mirror over your stove.
  - Keep the stove and oven clean and all burners working.

- Use all burners regularly.
- If the stove is next to the sink or dishwasher, place a wood or metal element between them.
- Don't store pans inside stove.

- Sink
  - Keep drains clean and fix leaky faucets.
  - Place a woody plant, fresh flowers, or a bowl of fruit somewhere between the stove and sink. If that's not possible, hang a crystal halfway between the stove and sink.
  - If you have a window over the sink, a green plant may add to the health of the family.

- Table
  - Use an even number of chairs at the table.
  - If possible, keep the table as far away from the cooking area as you can.
  - Place a live plant or a metal bowl of fruit in the center of the table.

- Don't seat anyone at the sharp corners of the table.
- Don't allow the table to block the kitchen entrance.
- Keep clutter off the table.
- The kitchen table is not a good place for bills.

5

The Bedroom

*S*tand in the doorway with your compass and Eight Directions Chart (see page 15 and really look at the room where you spend nearly a third of your life. The bedroom is where we rest, and replenish, where we make love, and conceive children, where we think about, and discuss, many of life's problems.

Lie down on your bed. Close your eyes for a moment, then open them. What do you see? Whatever it is, that is what the astral body will wake up to while you're sleeping. What if it has an effect on your dreams, on whether you sleep well or not?

You must decide what you want to get out of your sleep time and from all your time in the bedroom. Because my work is in a creative field, I want to dream. Many of my best ideas have come while my conscious mind rests. If you are having a health problem, look at the chart, see which directions and colors will enhance healing. If you are in a relationship dilemma, which colors, directions, and numbers can bring a solution? You've heard the old saying, "Sleep on it, and things will look better in the morning." If you're sleeping in a bedroom with healthy chi, that is certainly true.

How does one accomplish healthy, flowing chi in the bedroom? Often it can be accomplished simply by cleaning up and moving things around, and perhaps adding a few things.

Bedroom
Colors, Numbers, and Elements

Use the Eight Directions Chart and the Creative Cycle of Elements chart (see page 16) to aid you.

Look to the Destructive Cycle of Elements chart (see page 17) to see which arrangements to avoid. Placing certain elements together can disrupt the chi in your room.

Let's begin with the bed. Your head should lie in the direction that best suits your goal. If you are trying to conceive a child, consider the west for the head of the bed. If you're focusing on a new career, north would best.

If you can avoid it, do not have your bed aligned with a doorway. In the early days of Feng Shui, that was called the "death" position. When a person was gravely ill, they would move the bed closer to the door so when the individual died, it would be easier to remove the body. The most ideal location, then, is as far from the door as possible (see diagram on page 62). If you have a small bedroom and can't avoid a doorway, hang a crystal or two bamboo flutes from the ceiling, halfway between the bed and the doorway.

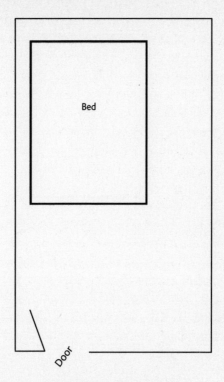

Bed

Door

WORST POSITION FOR BED

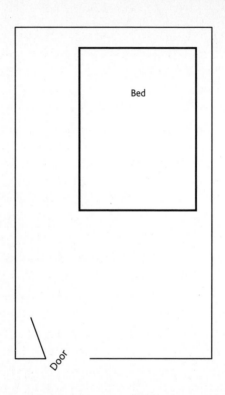

Bed

Door

IDEAL POSITION FOR BED

Many bedrooms have an adjacent bathroom. Since the bathroom is where a great deal of water drains away, having your bed aligned with it can drain not only your energy but your funds as well. Remember, the flow of water is associated with your finances. Even if your bathroom is on a story above or below, consider where it is in conjunction with your bed.

If you can't avoid having your bed near a bathroom, look to the colors and numbers on the Eight Directions Chart and use them accordingly. For instance, I have a small bedroom with a bathroom in the west. At this time, I am concerned with health issues, so the head of my bed is in the east, which aligns with the bathroom door. To counteract the negatives, I keep the door closed at night. I also hung a crystal halfway between the foot of my bed and the door. I mounted a mirror above the bathroom door, placed two green, woody plants on each side of the bed, and a landscape painting on the east wall. That gives me green, wood, and the number three in the east and a quick fix for the bathroom door.

Because the bedroom is where you are most vulnerable, where you practice the most intimate of acts, where your body heals and replenishes for the day to come, it's important to feel comfortable, safe, and relaxed there. The correct choice of wall colors, curtains, bedspreads, and furniture should enhance those feelings. You don't have to paint your walls all different colors for the optimal results. If you want a white bedroom, bring the necessary colors in through knickknacks, fabrics, pictures, wall hangings, and plants. Be mindful of the Cycle of Elements charts to ensure you have accomplished a creative cycle.

Try moving the dresser, or chest of drawers, to the east wall and place a green plant, with soft rounded leaves, on top. By adding a green candle on either side of the plant, you have positioned three green items in the correct direction for health concerns. Move that picture of flowers, with the splashes of red, to the south wall. If there are nine blooms, all the better; you have worked in the right color and number for the south.

If your child is having problems in school, place the head of his or her bed in the northeast. If there is a desk in the room, make sure it does not face the wall, and use containers made of earthenware or clay to hold pencils and other small desk items. Remember, it is important the desk is uncluttered. Only those things the child is working on should be on the desk. Statuary, planters, even a painting with turquoise in it, can be placed on a headboard or night table, or hung on the wall over the bed or desk. Or, you can string eight turquoise beads and hang them from a lamp, windowsill, or ceiling.

It's not as important to understand why Feng Shui works, as it is to try it and see the results. Move that bed, clean underneath it, change your artwork and knickknacks around, or use quick fixes, such as crystals, bamboo flutes, or mirrors to handle those things you can't accomplish in other ways. Think creatively. Check your closets, drawers, and things you have boxed away. You may be surprised at what you have that will help incorporate the right colors, numbers, and elements into your bedroom to bring about the desired results. Open your mind to the process, and be aware of what changes in your life. It will cost you next to nothing, in time and money, and it just might work.

Quick Tips for the Bedroom

- L-shaped room
  - If a sharp corner in the wall juts out, place a tall plant, an urn, a statue, or a standing mirror in front of it.
  - If you use a mirror, make sure it is not in line with the foot of your bed.
- One-room apartment
  - The southeast corner is best for the sleeping area.
  - Separate the area with a beaded curtain, some potted plants, or a folding screen. If none are available, a coffee table or other long piece of furniture will work.
- Bed
  - If your bed is a pull-out couch, try to place it against a southeast wall and incorporate tips for the living room.
  - Position the bed as far from the entrance to the room as possible.

- With a king bed, if the box spring consists of two pieces, bring them together with a fitted sheet or a piece of fabric or a blanket large enough to tuck in. Red is best. It's easy to dye a sheet.
- The bed should not be in line with the doorway or block the doorway. If it is or does, hang a crystal, chimes, or two bamboo flutes between the bed and the door.
- The best bed position is as far from the door as possible.
- Place the bed against a solid wall. If there is a window, put a night table between the bed and the wall.
- Make sure your head is not pointed toward the bathroom or kitchen. Those areas can drain chi. Use a standing mirror at the head of the bed, or set a small mirror and two white candles on a bookcase-style headboard.

- Do not store things under the bed. If you must, attach a small mirror to the foot and the side of the bed frame to reflect chi around the bed.
- Ceiling
  - If you have a beamed ceiling, positioning a canopy over the bed, or suspending two bamboo flutes from the beam over your bed, can cancel the ill effects of the beams.
  - If you have an angled ceiling, hang a crystal from the lower side of the ceiling.
  - If you have a ceiling fan, suspend a crystal from the fan's pull string.
- Other furnishings and equipment
  - If a piece of furniture has sharp corners, make sure it's positioned so the corners don't point at you while you're in bed. If it's unavoidable, cover the corners with fabric that extends over the corners.

- Do not place a mirror at the foot of bed. If you must, cover it at night.
- Close the curtains at night. If you don't wish to close them, hang crystals in the windows instead.
- Try to keep electronic equipment out of the bedroom, or at least cover the screens at night.
- Any type of work or exercise equipment should be covered or hidden behind a screen at night.

6

The Bathroom

*T*he bathroom shouldn't take long. After all, you can't move your toilet, sink, and tub or shower. However, there are some practical Feng Shui concepts and fixes that work well in this most private room.

When bathrooms were moved from the outside into the home, at first they were simply functional rooms. In our busy world today, the bathroom may be the one place where one can find solitude, where the phone, television, kids, pets, and other distractions can be put aside for a short time. If the bathroom is your place of peace, perhaps you should consider an atmosphere that lends itself to a feeling of peace.

The main element in any bathroom is water. Since a great deal of water is flushed, or drained through the tub and sink, we must be careful not to allow chi to be drained with it. Besides keeping your bathroom clean, since germs spread easily there, keep the toilet lid closed when flushing or not in use, and plug your sink and tub when not in use. If you do nothing else, remember these two things.

In my research, I read that the bathroom shouldn't be too spacious. One can only dream. It seems I always end up with a bathroom so small I can sit on the toilet, wash my feet, and brush my teeth at the same time. I really don't believe a bathroom's size should be that important. After all, you can't shrink it, and why would you want to? It's more important to make it a relaxing place, whether it's large or small.

The best location for a bathroom is along an outside wall but not too close to your front entrance or the kitchen. Even if it is not in an ideal location, there are ways to apply Feng Shui.

Bathroom
Colors, Numbers, and Elements

With the bathroom, you'll be doing the best you can with the space you have and with the way the tub, sink, and toilet are already laid out. Like the other rooms in the house, when using numbers and colors, look to the Eight Directions Chart (see page 15) for optimal success. You must first know what your main concern is when you spend time in the bathroom. Are you concerned most with health, wealth, travel, family issues, or business? Keep in mind that without health and good digestion, life can seem pretty bleak—and all the wealth in the world won't bring you that wonderful feeling you have when the body is healthy and vital.

Quick Tips for the Bathroom

- Location and layout
  - The best position is along an outside wall, away from the front entrance and kitchen. If the bathroom is not in the best position, hang a mirror outside the bathroom door.
  - Hang a crystal or chimes to mitigate sharp wall corners that point at a person. A tall plant can be used instead.
  - Beams overhead can cause discord. Two hollow bamboo flutes will cancel it out.
- Toilet
  - The toilet is best placed behind the door; it should not be visible from the door.
  - If it is visible from the door, put something between the door and the toilet to disguise it, or attach a small mirror to the base of the toilet.

- Colors
  - Restful colors such as green can help digestion. If your walls are not green, you could add green towels or plants.
  - Blue in the bathroom will be helpful if you have plumbing problems.
- Decor
  - Candles can bring a bit of fire into the atmosphere. They help with balancing the large volume of water flowing through the bathroom.
  - If it's a student's bathroom, consider turquoise towels or bathroom accessories, or string eight turquoise beads and hang them in the northeast section of the room.
  - If your focus is on a new career, try placing a black statue or an onyx stone in the north.

- If you are involved in a creative endeavor, position a painting with a splash of red or orange on a south wall.
- Pleasing, restful artwork in wooden frames will add balance to your room. Do not place pictures of water on a south wall.

7

The Home Office

Whether you have a desk in your living room for paying bills or you run a business or work in your home office, the placement of the desk is most important. When you sit at your desk, you should face the open room and your back should be toward a wall, not the door (see diagram on page 82). This was a problem for me because I write at a seven-foot-tall secretary. Even if I could move it away from a wall, I couldn't see around it. My Feng Shui fix was to hang a mirror on the cabinet door above my typewriter so I could see the door behind me and another on the wall to my left so I could see the rest of the room.

My husband's computer desk is in one end of the living room. Since it is a rectangular desk, we turned it around so he can see the entire room and its doors. It's an old desk and the back was not very attractive, so we hung a colorful serape to hide the back and placed a chair in front of it. Now it is in a more commanding position.

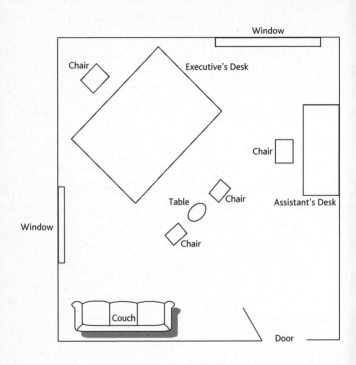

Window

Chair

Executive's Desk

Chair

Assistant's Desk

Table

Chair

Window

Chair

Couch

Door

Best Placement for Desk

If you have a separate home office located in the south, it should enhance fame, fortune, and success. The northeast is best for knowledge and scholarly endeavors. If your office is in part of another room, try to place the desk in an area that is conducive to what you wish to achieve. For instance, if you are a creative designer, writer, or artist, south would be great. If you are in school or doing more practical work at your desk, northeast would be suitable. By paying attention to the Eight Directions Chart (see page 15), you'll see that red helps the creative cycle and shades of blues and greens or turquoise can aid in more scholarly projects.

The first step is to decide what the main purpose of your office is. Then place the desk in its most commanding position for that purpose, and go from there.

Home Office
Colors, Numbers, and Elements

If your office is in a separate room, and it is where you conduct business or where you work at home, you will want to pay close attention to the Cycle of Elements charts (see page 16–17) and arrange items to enhance a creative cycle. Even if your desk is made of wood, it might help to put a green plant on the desktop or a large plant next to the desk. An aquarium or fountain can bring the water element to the room, but if you don't have them, a seashell, some sea salt in a small container, or a picture of water will work. Metal can usually be found in office equipment.

Even if your desk is part of another room, it should be considered in the Cycle of Elements charts. Look at the entire room. Are you building a creative cycle with the office area included?

If your office equipment is in the southeast, which is your wealth corner, why not include four purple items to enhance your chances for wealth and fortune? The four items could be as simple as purple stones, flowers, pictures with purple in them, or fish in a bowl with a purple cloth beneath it. Use your imagination.

If you're starting a new career, try a black statue in the north corner of your desk, or a picture with black in it on a north wall. But pay attention to the materials your statue or picture frame is made of; make sure they align with the Cycle of Elements charts.

Know what your motivation is in your office and pick your colors, elements, and numbers accordingly. What if you could make better choices, be more informed, get your creative juices flowing simply by adding a few things, moving that desk, or cleaning out old clutter?

Quick Tips for the Home Office

- Desk and equipment
  - Don't sit with your back to the room or door. If it's unavoidable, hang mirrors to reflect the door and the room.
  - Windows should be to the side of the desk. If there is glare, hang a crystal in the window.
  - Avoid clutter. Keep on the desktop only what you are working on.
  - Don't place the desk under the low end of a sloped ceiling. If you must, put a floor lamp next to it that shines upward.
  - Office equipment should be positioned in the west or southwest corner, but check the best direction for your goal.
- Storage
  - Bookcases are best enclosed. If they aren't, keep them clean and uncluttered with old business.

- Make sure no sharp corners are pointed toward you. If it's unavoidable, arrange a potted vine so that it drapes over the corners.

8

Foyers, Hallways, and Stairs

*S*teep staircases, spiral staircases, blocked foyers, and narrow, dark hallways can affect the flow of chi to other rooms. One thing all three have in common is lighting. Poor lighting not only can affect your chi but can also cause accidents. None of these areas are good for storage or clutter either. If the flow of energy is stopped in the foyer, sits at the bottom of a steep staircase, or slides down a staircase too quickly, then it can't get to the rest of the house, and the other rooms will suffer. A cluttered hallway with too much furniture can hold your chi hostage until it is of no use. You must keep it moving, but slowly enough to nourish the living space. It's just like taking care of our bodies. What good would it do to eat if the food didn't stay in us long enough to nourish our essential organs?

Foyers
Colors, Numbers, and Elements

To assess your foyer, walk outside and walk back in. What is your first impression? That will tell you what changes need to be made, if any. When a guest arrives for the first time, steps into your foyer and states that they just love your house, you know you have achieved the right Feng Shui for that area.

Quick Tips for Foyers

- If you have a wall within six to eight feet of the door, hang a large mirror or a scenic picture on it.

- Remove clutter. Use a coatrack or coat tree
  to keep jackets and hats out of the way. For
  shoes, a shoe rack or basket works as long as
  it is not in the way.
- If you have a larger foyer, keep furnishings
  simple and sparse. A small round table with
  a plant or vase or flowers on it is inviting.
- A sharp-cornered wall can be softened with
  a potted plant.
- The color of your foyer should reflect what
  you want a person's first impression of your
  house to be. Try to stay away from stark
  colors.

Hallways
Colors, Numbers, and Elements

If there are things in your hallway you must walk
around, or a piece of furniture you continu-
ally bump into, your chi has to do the same.

The hallway feeds nourishment to the rest of your rooms, so it must be kept in good order and clear of debris. Colors and artwork should give a person a feeling of peace as they look for rooms beyond the hallway. Hallways are not as goal-oriented as rooms; they are about the journey to your goal. You must decide how you want to proceed on your journey.

Quick Tips for Hallways

- General
  - For L-shaped hallways, at the point where the hallway turns, place a small, round table or a potted plant in the sharp corner, or hang a crystal there.
  - Watch your cycle elements. If you have too much fire in a hallway, the chi could move so fast it misses other rooms.
  - A pole light will fix any dark areas and attract good chi.

- Narrow hallway
  - Keep it well lit and clear of clutter.
  - Lay a runner with a vertical pattern to move chi faster; with a horizontal pattern to slow it down.
  - Suspend a crystal from the ceiling halfway down the hallway.
  - Hang a mirror at the far end to encourage chi to flow all the way down the hall.
- Hallway doors
  - If your main hallway has doors to other rooms, keep the doors unobstructed by furniture.
  - Doors and knobs should be in good repair.
  - Leave doors open, if possible. If you don't want to leave doors completely open, leave them cracked open.
  - A small wind chime that hits the top of an opening door will help chi move into

the other rooms.
- Growing plants near a door will bring
  chi to the doorway.

Stairs
Colors, Numbers, and Elements

Pay close attention to staircases and steps; if they
are difficult for you to navigate, they will be difficult for your chi as well. Make sure they are
sturdy, safe, well lit, and free of shoes, clothes,
boxes, or anything else that inhibits your journey—or that of your chi—up and down the staircase or steps.

Quick Tips for Stairs

- Spiral staircase
  - Keep well lit at both ends.
  - Place live plants at the bottom or
    beneath the staircase.

- Paint the handrail so it looks like a plant growing upward.
- If possible, hang a painting of pooled water near the bottom of the staircase.
- Tie a green ribbon at the base, at the center, and at the top of the handrail.
- Be careful what color you paint a spiral staircase. Like the hallway, it is about the journey, not a goal.

- Wide staircase
  - If the staircase is straight, add potted plants, ceramic pottery, or statues to give it a more curved appearance.
  - A mirror at the landing will keep the chi from pooling there.
  - Potted plants on both sides of the foot of a wide staircase will keep the chi from flowing down too fast.
  - Small guide lights embedded in the steps will keep the chi flowing.

- Steps
  - For a steep staircase, hang a crystal at the foot and a mirror on the landing to help the chi flow upwards.
  - If you have a few steps leading down to a sunken room, hang a crystal at the top and place a floor lamp that shines upward at the bottom, which also helps lift up the sunken room.
  - For steps leading upstairs, a chime will help chi move to the room above.

9   *Goals and Fixes*

From health to relationships and careers, there are many reasons people are drawn to Feng Shui. If you have a specific problem you wish to work on, begin in that particular area of your living space that corresponds to the issue. If you are trying to bring the family closer together, seek more honest communications, your focus should be on the dining area and living room. If you want to conceive a child, rejuvenate a relationship, or bring more passion into your life, begin in the bedroom. If you are career oriented or concerned about the flow of funds, concentrate on the work areas and wealth corners of your living space.

It is a simple matter of becoming aware of the problem areas of your life and consulting the Eight Directions and Cycle of Elements charts to improve the flow of chi in your space and increase the peace, health, harmony, and abundance in your life. The following table provides a quick reference to the potential problem areas in your life and their Feng Shui solutions.

Solutions at a Glance

Issues: Health, Family
Direction: East
Element: Wood
Season: Spring
Number: 3
Color: Green
Solutions:

- All metal removed from the area
- Enhanced with live plants, silk plants, or images of plants

- Hues of green and blue in furnishings, walls, and accessories
- For water energy, a fountain or pictures depicting water, seashells, sea salt, or a watering can

Issues: Prosperity, Wealth
Direction: Southeast
Element: Wood
Season:
Number: 4
Color: Purple
Solutions:

- Large, woody plants, or plants with purple blossoms; the darker the leaves, the better
- Wind chimes
- Goldfish, real or fake, or a picture of goldfish
- Pictures or statuary having to do with prosperity

- Shades of purple and green
- A wealth corner with four purple items

Issues: Fame, Fortune, Creativity
Direction: South
Element: Fire
Season: Summer
Number: 9
Color: Red
Solutions:

- Red candles, pictures with splashes of red, red figurines, red throw pillows, perhaps one red wall
- Red fabric under your telephone
- Crystals that cast rainbows into the room
- Pointed objects or plants with pointed or spiked leaves, especially plants with red blossoms
- Real wood to feed the fire: wood frames, figurines, planters, or woody plants

- Displays of awards, diplomas, and press releases
- A picture of a celebrity who does what you want to be famous for

⋘⃝

Issues: Relationships, Motherhood
Direction: Southwest
Element: Earth
Season:
Number: 2
Color: Yellow and Pink
Solutions:

- Basic earth tones in soft fabrics, with accents in yellow and pink
- Soft lighting and scented candles
- Pictures of pairs: pairs of candles, two flowering plants, and so on
- A round mirror

⋘⃝

Issues: Purity, Conception
Direction: West
Element: Metal
Season: Autumn
Number: 7
Color: White
Solutions:

- Uncluttered area in shades of white in walls, furnishings, or accents
- Soft curves and shapes in furnishings; natural fabrics
- Crystal hung over head at work, or over bed if trying to conceive a child
- Metal accents supported by ceramic pieces and round-leaved plants
- White flowers and candles
- Metal-framed picture depicting your goal

Issues: Friends, Travel, Benefactors, Fatherhood
Direction: Northwest

Element: Metal

Season:

Number: 6

Color: Gray

Solutions:

- Shades of white in walls or furnishings; can be done with accent pieces
- To open the area: no clutter, sparse furniture
- Metal frames, statuary, flowerpots, metal and glass end tables
- Crystals and white flowers, or plants with white blooms
- Ceramic pots, to give the earth element to support metal
- To counteract too much metal, a splash of red in an accent piece, and a water element: a fountain, picture, small fishbowl, or seashells, especially white shells

Issues: Career, Death
Direction: North
Element: Water
Season: Winter
Number: 1
Color: Black
Solutions:

- Accents with dark shades of blue or black with a hint of red, such as a black vase with red flowers
- Fountains or aquariums
- Pictures with bodies of water in them
- Picture depicting something in your chosen career field
- Something metal to enhance your water
- A live plant to encourage growth

⁓◐)

Issues: Self-knowledge, Scholarly success
Direction: Northeast
Element: Earth

Season:
Number: 8
Color: Turquoise
Solutions:

- Earth tones on walls, furnishings, and accessories
- Natural fabrics
- Soft, inviting chairs and sofas
- Large statues and accent pieces made of ceramic or stone
- Table lamps instead of overhead lighting
- Religious figurines
- Meditation spot
- Full-length mirror
- Desk for studying, with crystal hung above chair and a bit of red near desk
- Flowering plants with yellow or orange in flowers or leaves

just
try
this

Afterword

Our living space is a reflection of our body and soul. No matter how big or small our living space is, how we take care of it can affect our lives. Feng Shui is about not only balance but also awareness and perspective. It's an aid to help us find our path in life, reach our goals, dare to dream.

Chi, the energy that flows through our space, is the lifeblood of our home. If you had problems with the blood flow in your body and were told there was a cure for it, wouldn't you try it? If the cure brought you from an exhausted, depressed, nonfunctioning person to a thriving, vital one, wouldn't it be worth the effort?

And Feng Shui does not have to be a difficult cure. Its basic principles work in any living space. Is it possible to apply Feng Shui to a house in one day? I did it. We live in an eight-room house, with two and a half levels that wander up the side of a mountain. It's an old house, but it has great character. After getting the house cleaned, I began the process. Armed with crystals, bamboo flutes, chimes, candles, and a knowledge of what was already available in the house, I shut off the phone, turned off the television, chased everyone out, and went through the house like a whirlwind.

At the entrance to each room, I consulted my compass, checked the Eight Directions and Cycle of Elements charts, moved what needed to be moved and used quick fixes for what couldn't be moved. I shifted a painting depicting water from the south wall to the north and three plants to the east, hung a mirror at the top of the staircase and flutes over a bed in a room with a beamed ceiling, arranged two red candles in the south near my working area. You get the idea. After doing the first room, it became easier to tell the direction, to know what to do. The rooms felt good, and I felt good.

Scoff if you must, but things started happening—not a month or a year later, but right away. A serious health issue was resolved, a book deal I'd been waiting months for came through, my creativity became energized through dreaming. And it continues. Since then, I've shared Feng Shui with friends and relatives and heard wonderful stories about the changes in their lives.

So why not give Feng Shui a try? You have nothing to lose, and it just might work. You don't really need to understand its origins, or why it works, or how it works. All you need is the willingness to try it and see if it works for you. Even if you don't think it enhanced your life, at least you'll end up with a clean house and the knowledge of a new tool you can use when you are ready for a change.

A crystal hung in the window might not bring you money, but it can bring you a wealth of good feeling in the form of rainbows dancing across the room. It's one of those things that make you smile when no one else is there to see.

About the Author

Barb Rogers is a professional costume designer, founder of Broadway Bazaar Costumes, and the author of two costuming books. She is also the writer/creator of *Mystic Glyphs: An Oracle Based on Native American Symbols*. She lives in Arizona with her husband and two dogs.

To Our Readers

Red Wheel, an imprint of Red Wheel/Weiser,
publishes books on topics ranging from spunky
self-help, spirituality, personal growth, and
relationships to women's issues and social issues.
Our mission is to publish quality books that will
make a difference in people's lives—how we feel
about ourselves and how we relate to one another
and to the world at large. We value integrity,
compassion, and receptivity, both in the books
we publish and in the way we do business.

Our readers are our most important resource,
and we value your input, suggestions, and ideas
about what you would like to see published. Please
feel free to contact us, to request our latest book
catalog, or to be added to our mailing list.

Red Wheel/Weiser, LLC
P.O. Box 612
York Beach, ME 03910-0612
www.redwheelweiser.com